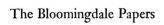

The Bloomingdale Papers

Also by Hayden Carruth

HAYDEN CARRUTH

The Bloomingdale Papers

The University of Georgia Press, Athens

In the exiled poet's room
Where Fear and the Muse keep watch by turn
while night comes on
that has no hope of dawn . . .

Akhmatova

Explanation and Apology, Twenty Years After

Toward the end of summer in 1953, after years of acute illness, I suffered a final collapse—at least it seemed final at the time—and ended up in White Plains at the psychiatric branch of New York Hospital, still known familiarly at that time by the name it had had from its founding in the eighteenth century until about 1935: Bloomingdale. It was a huge old asylum; a private asylum, less grisly in some respects than public asylums like Bellevue or Wingdale, but grisly enough and decidedly old-fashioned. Those were the days before widespread use of tranquilizers and other chemotherapy. Shuffleboard, handicrafts, and tepid baths (in special tanks with a canvas jacket to hold the bather), together with occasional consultations with a doctor, were still regarded as good enough treatment even for deep psychosis, and when these failed the usual recourse was to shock and sometimes to isolation. At all events I remained in the admissions ward for about two months and was then transferred to the convalescent ward, where I was led to expect I would spend two or three more months, thereupon to graduate to the open ward for a similar period and go on to eventual discharge. I was mystified by all this because I could see no change whatever in my state of being nor make any sense of the things I was required to do; but part of my illness was a need to do what I was told (in anger and under protest), so I did it. One of the doctors suggested that since I called myself a writer I should write something that might be helpful to him and his colleagues in their consideration of my case, the idea being, I suppose, that I might be more articulate on paper than I was in speech. As a result, for a couple of hours each day while the other patients were occupied elsewhere, I sat in my cell with a portable typewriter and wrote. What I turned out was the poem, or sequence of poems, in this book.

In January of the following year I suffered a further breakdown and was transferred to Hall Seven, the ward for chronic cases. Thereafter I wrote no more. I was subjected to a series of electroshock treatments, which affected my memory, but aside from this and aside from watching the McCarthy hearings on TV, my only accomplishment during many months on Hall Seven was playing 1500 games of solitaire and keeping a record of the number that came out. I can assure anyone who wants to know that solitaire is a losing game. Sometimes too, for "administrative" reasons, I was sent for short periods to Hall Five, the ward for senile patients and others similarly bemused. Eventually I left the hospital, though in worse shape than when I had entered it, and slipped into a period of phobic isolation which lasted . . . but that is another story.

It is difficult now to reconstruct the events relating to my poem. Apparently I did more work on it after I left the hospital because a few excerpts from it, revised and improved, were included in my first book, *The Crow and the Heart* (1959). At some point, I think before I left the hospital, a carbon copy of the entire manuscript, which my wife had retyped, was given to my old friend Albert Christ-Janer. For my part I completely forgot about the poem—a lapse which I believe can be ascribed, like many others, to the effects of electroshock—so that when Albert turned up his copy recently and showed it to the editors of the University of Georgia Press, and when they in turn wrote to me to say they would like to publish it, I had no idea what they were talking about. I had to ask them to send me the manuscript. When it came I read it and recognized it—with dismay. My first inclination was to burn it. All that stiffness, awkwardness, phony diction, that tight-lipped psychopathic compression: it seemed appalling. And I still have misgivings about publication. I agree to it partly because friends have persuaded me I should, partly because I have the impression from reading the whole poem that in spite of the bad writing—in some sense even because of it—the total effect is what it should be, the truth of a spirit caged and struggling. Readers should remember that for people in certain crises of disintegrating personality the act of writing, or of making any utterance, is a self-assertion entailing risks literally tantamount to death, so that every word must be forced out willfully and then controlled with rigid, disguising care. This is the emotional matrix of the poem. I think it gives to the language a certain expressive force, but if I am wrong I apologize. In other matters I feel no need for apology. I should like to ward off, for example, the label of "confessional" that may be applied to the poem by analogy to others published during the past twenty years. The poem is not that. When I wrote it I was in no condition to confess anything, if the term means more than merely mythopoetic autobiography, and I am not sorry; there has been plenty of confession elsewhere. Nor am I sorry that my poem fails to deal more dramatically with the miseries I and my friends suffered in the hospital, the privation, hopelessness, violence, tears, the terrific pain, and above all the humiliation. There has been plenty of that elsewhere too, and the ambience here can be taken for granted. Instead my poem seems to me lyric and elegiac, and though the materials of it are my own experience it is impersonal. (It was no help at all to the doctors.) I think of it as a paradigm of the general quality of life in this country during the 1950s.

As for the work's antecedents, the last major poems I had read before entering the hospital were Pound's *Pisan Cantos* and Williams's *Paterson*, with both of which I had been deeply and positively engaged as editor and reviewer. But I had also been close to other American poets whose writings were of a different kind, especially Allen Tate and J. V. Cunningham; and close too, again as editor, publisher, etc., to the whole "atmosphere" of American verse circa 1950, so alien to today's. I have a memory, vague, of reading Charles Olson's "Projective Verse" in *Poetry New York* and some poems of his in *ViVa* (was it?), but the force of what was happening at Black Mountain had not reached me in 1953, and of course the ferment associated with Allen Ginsberg and Jack Kerouac was still to come. All I can safely say is that I was, like many others, dissatisfied with what then seemed the common course of American poetry and with the way it had deviated from the work of earlier masters, while at the same time I was struck by the poetic values I found in very diverse models. In other words I was as confused in matters of poetry as I was in everything else. It shows in what I wrote. But I believed—and still do, against the curse of eclecticism my friends lay on me—that manners are ultimately reducible to substance, in poetry as in life, and that what works, works.

Some things in the poem can be explained by my awareness that the first people who would read it, and probably the last, were the doctors, whose way of thinking I often found very different from my own. This applies to the defense of poetry on page 6, for instance. Beyond this I should make note of the persons who were in my mind while I was writing, aside from those I saw every day in the hospital: my first wife, from whom I had been divorced for about two years and whose loss I still deeply regretted; our small daughter; my second wife, a very beautiful young woman toward whom, in our forced separation, I looked with feelings of dependence, great affection, and half-suppressed guilt; my parents; and my various doctors, both those in the hospital and those who had treated me previously, one of whom had been a woman. I should mention also that in the case of the few excerpts which were published in *The Crow and the Heart* I have substituted those improved versions in this printing of the entire poem. It would be silly to publish inferior versions just for the sake of chronological authenticity, especially since *The Crow and the Heart* is now out of print. Otherwise the impossibility of reentering work so remote from my present has restrained me from attempting major changes, though in retyping the manuscript I could not resist modifying punctuation and diction in some passages and inserting minor clarifications in others. The title also is new, and so is the epigraph, which I have adapted from another poet's translation of Anna Akhmatova's "Voronezh," a poem written for and about Osip Mandelstam. In using this epigraph I do not mean to suggest an analogy between Mandelstam's Siberia and my Bloomingdale—that would be highly improper—but rather to point to the inner condition of exile as the experience *par excellence* of the mid-twentieth century. The line quoted on page 42 is from a poem by Louise Bogan, whom I had known before I entered the hospital. She herself had once done time in Bloomingdale, and she wrote me several letters of encouragement while I was there, letters which I'm afraid I never answered. Other quotations from older poets are given without quotation marks. As for the quatrain on page 50 that does have quotation marks, I cannot remember if it was taken from another poet or if I wrote it myself, but I suspect the latter. Only one further point needs expansion; on page 6 are four names, Bob, Old Tom, Young Enrico, and Poor Jan. Respectively they are Robert Hutchins, chancellor of the university; St. Thomas Aquinas; Enrico Fermi; and Jan Masaryk, whose monumental statue at one end of the Midway presided over the university neighborhood.

Bloomingdale was in old times the name of an entire section of New York. The Dutch called it Bloomendael— the Vale of Flowers.

Of course I have written a number of other poems about what happened to me in Bloomingdale. In fact I think my original purpose in writing the sequence called "The Asylum" (first published in *The Crow and the Heart* and later in *For You*) was to condense and give firmer objective structure to these materials from the hospital, and there have been several later poems, including some quite recent. A few of these may be, if not better poems, at least more in line with current tastes. But the long poem done in the hospital was the generator of them all; never elsewhere was that actuality so close to me. I'm glad I got it on paper when I did. Looking back at it I am overcome by mixed feelings, as one is when confronted by one's former self: shame for the callowness, bitterness for the suffering, resentment for the loss, and at the same time a kind of admiration for the spirit that endured. But chiefly I am relieved. Thank God it's over.

H.C.

29 June 1973

Addendum on proof. With sorrow I must record the death of Albert Christ-Janer on December 12, 1973. He was killed in an auto crack-up in the mountains of northern Italy, on his way back to Bellagio after a day of painting alone in the high country. If death can ever be fitting, at least the manner of his, in its clarity and toughness, fitted well with the manner of his life. He was a loyal friend, a sensitive, intelligent artist, an honest man; and although originally I did not think this book could be dedicated to anyone in particular, I should like now to inscribe it publicly to him: Albert Christ-Janer, 1910-1973, *in memoriam*.

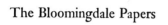

The Bloomingdale Papers

IT ALL BEGINS on this November day.
The wintertime realities are thin.

The trees are gaunt and gray and weaving black;
The earth is brown; the grass is dry and frayed.

Old summer's lifeless leaves contrive a sea
That sweeps beyond the hedge and floods the gate,

And scant waves are withdrawing from the hill,
Rattling like tides on stony, desolate shores.

A windblown plume leaps on the tennis court,
Where the causeless air moves many ways at once.

An oak on the hill still clings to its russet leaves;
Below, two hemlocks touch with somber arms.

One scarcely notices the north bank's beauty,
The moss in its mosaic, subtle, soft,

Byzantine in green and gray. And the ivy gibbers
Against the wall, discourse of auld lang syne.

Only an image ago huge puffs of green,
Tribes of birds, cities of crickets and ants,

And the tumbling sun made jocund all our eyes.
That was the jeweled time, that was summer.

1

Now even the corpses have vanished. Sleeping trees
And one squirrel huddled against the wind

In the deserted suburb of a maple
Are two of the remembrances of life.

The light, though, is the chief ubiquity.
It has no wash, no flow; it is so thin

It cancels distance and this is Cézanne's world:
Our vision glides on objects in a plane.

This light is colorless. Perhaps it's gray.
But light achieves so many rich enticements:

Golden, as in the webs of an August noon;
Purple, as in the shadow of a cliff;

Pellucid rose, as in September twilight;
White, as moondrift gleams on the world of snow.

This time is lightless, but not dark nor dim.
The sky is gray, but it is not a sky,

The reassuring arc is gone. The slope
And jut of earth, the trees, the seas of leaves,

These make a low relief, and some deep grain
Of deeper stone shows through the flat, dull air.

But wintertime realities are thin,
And easily, easily we neglect their seeming.

Instead this time of winter, this faint time,
Is the fallen year, the turning in. Far off

I know there is a country where we go
Only adventuresomely, where the bears
With summer in their bellies sink to sleep,
Abatement, a subsidence of the will
Into warm lures and ardors of their dreams.
And here the wind veers to the cold northeast.
Another oak leaf makes a silent parting
And circles downward like a swinging gull
To the sea below. And everywhere this is
The time for shoulder-turning carelessly
After a pondering glance, the withdrawing time,
Time for the turning in and inward, time
For the long, long scrutabilities of the fire.
So rich and fearful are the dreams of winter
We never mourn the filmy world outside,
We even turn our anger from the door
That opens only for someone else's key
And from the windows and their iron bars.
Prison grows warm and *is* the real asylum.
And all the terrors of our inward journeys,
The grave indecencies, the loathsome birds,
Are goads to the strange bravery we muster,
We crippled, unbrave ones; and our hard days
Become as perilous as our quilted nights.
Into quiescence we pursue our killers;
Into fell lassitude we fight our way.
And never in our drowsy eyes appears
For an instant any boredom but the sharp
Unwearying tedium of this great despair.
These are the fascinations of our winter.

Our lives are close and iron-girt; we thread
Among the phantoms of this narrowed world,
We trolls and banshees, with our special ears
Keen for the murmurs that so insidiously

Lurk in a sounding skull. The wheatworm works,
The weevil, the caterpillar, the ked, the tick—
Alive in the flimsy center, turning, turning.
The tiny webs of sight and sound give way,
The little chaos thickens, blur by blur,
And soon the nest of consciousness is loosed,
The straws and twigs and downy feathers tumbled.
And the bird is dead among the dancing worms,
And all the world pours down the cliff of dreams.

The rare saint writ "that it behooveth thee
To lead a dying life," thereby to reach
In life a little the extraordinary
Aspirings of the spirit after death.
Another, somewhat apprehensively,
Though I shall grudge no man his manner, spoke
Of "inner freedom from the practical desire."
And many more men likewise if less well.
Now I should be the last to say that we
In this quite specifiable asylum
Have managed any such deliverance.
No, all the learned doctors are agreed
And always have been: this is not release,
But possession, seizure, passion. Therapy
Was simply and expressly exorcism
In times whose gilded meanings still transport us,
And who shall say the method is disproved?
The worm I spoke of wasn't just their fancy.
We are its captives, sick and sore. But still
Some aspects of the mystic's regimen
Enter our lives. How else is it the world
Outside becomes Mongolia and these walls
Enclose a monastery? Say it is
A black religion if you like, an art,
Built on a failed hope, a sickening faith.

No one reads our meanings with an eye
So ready as ours to mark an obelus.
But there are curious analogies.
Are we the acted on, or are we actors?
Deprived, or have we in ourselves renounced?
Is our prismatic vision not a way
Of seeing what the guru sees in his
Embracing stare? "There is a pleasure sure
In being mad which none but madmen know."
Madmen? Oh seers, hiders, invalids,
You sports and errors, you who wash your hands,
And you who touch, you pilgrims, you deserters,
All frips and frumps and nonnies, all my friends
Who study the mirror's prophecy of murder,
Whose mirroring eyes give back each other's terror—
Take up your sainthood! You who know the sting
Of a beloved lie, who shiver for
The sandy grate of evil in your veins,
Yours is an insight of the real world.
And quietly you move your eyes away
Into the beveled vistas of the stars,
The greater order and the gist of night.
You fight for goodness in the swift, deep heart.
Mongolia shimmers like the shift of sand
On the wasted plains of the west; it will be swept
Away, or it will not; it does not matter.
Here in the round of our most private duty
Where the bell informs the changes of our day
We carry on our study and compose
The stanzas of our prayer. We learn to wear
With grace the tremor of an outraged hand.
We learn the dying life, and we are free,
Almost, from practical desire. We learn
The winning loss, the loser's peace, the toil
Of the idle, and the real world of dreams.

Such are the speculations of this winter.
The world hangs like an arras round this stage,
Woven in faded colors. November lays
The scene for pastoral. And randomly
My thoughts revolve to form this comedy.

✦

Let no imponderable lie
Transfix the sweetness of the eye,
Nor any waywardness command
A murder in the tranquil hand.
Only an honest gentleness
Of body binds the mind's distress.

✦

I am a poet
          whereby I mean no boast.
                                I want to
say simply, I am a poet, not a good one,
whereby neither do I mean any abasement.
      Poetry is profuse and multinominal
the latency of action
                 hence the polemics
and the modulations of wrath
even at the University of Chicago
                 where Bob introduced us to
                 Old Tom and Young Enrico
                 and Poor Jan looked on.
But poetry is at least
a manner of thinking
               one among many
a manner of perceiving
a manner of remembering
               one among many
it is no less respectable than landscape gardening for instance

it is for both writers and readers
poetry is in fact not so effective as one hopes
nor was it ever
                but one does one's best.
I choose this verse because it is natural to me
natural, I say, natural
                and the hell with you.

        Although sometimes I am abused by
the idea of prose
                the spirit of the age
I should think it easier
        but the prosaists say not
I should think it plainer
                the chief virtue
        but the newspapers testify to the contrary.

Let me say
with the levelness and intensity of deep feeling
I write in verse
        because I esteem fitness
        because I have an anticipation of beauty
and fitness and beauty are necessary to this task.

Of course how small I grow, weak, clumsy!
but my masters, you dead and you living
        I must work alone.

Thalia! guide me
dress thou my large conceits in simpleness
lend to my saying thy clarity and thy smile
give to my indecisions thine assurance
my little powers raise
my craft uplift
enter this solitude and comfort me
        in the darkness of my labor

1

Poets who sing our fear
Too often celebrate
The day's loss to the year.

A pending, general fate
They sing, and an abstract hurt.
Fear turns to opiate.

Yet some words still assert
The tongue's most ancient taste
Of fear. To eat the dirt

Of loving wakes a chaste
Old panic in the mind.
There is not any waste

Of fear among the blind
Who in a quiet street
Hear quicken from behind

The leopard's puffy feet.

1

'Tis a fine deceit
To pass away in a dream; indeed, I've slept
With mine eyes open a great while.

As for myself, I walk abroad o' nights.

But I went into Arabia and returned again unto Damascus.

What are those blue remembered hills,
    What spires, what farms are those?

8

Surely some revelation is at hand.

1

In the hot high summer I came.
The heaven fumed, the earth seethed,
The leaves of the trees hung heavily,
So many moist hands.
For ten days we lived in a cauldron.
So it seemed.
From the hot food
We turned away.
And I was under constant observation, as we say:
I couldn't take my dull stomach
Off to the healing solitude of sorrow.
Or my dull heart.
Misery was deep and everywhere
Like a sea smothering us.
And even now I ask how I came here.
The shock, looking up to see these bars.
We, the new ones, milled elusively,
Watching each other for the dangerous sign,
Wondering who among us was the one who was truly mad.
And the heat burned through the night,
As burned the attendant's light where he watched,
Through the night spying our shudders,
Hearing our sighs;
And sleep was the gift of a sullen queen.
The night broke with a scream, not mine.
But the possibility terrified me.
My belts and neckties were numbered and locked up at night,
My glasses taken away.
"Won't you play bridge?" asked the nurses.
"Checkers?" "Shuffleboard?" "Croquet?"
And the heat burned on through September.

The sky was a haze, a muslin blue.
At the beginning you are harried by examiners.
There is letting of blood, collecting of urine;
Psychologists, neurologists, urologists,
And the men who do ears, noses, and throats
Assemble upon you. You are thumped;
You are peered at, into, up; you are listened to.
Do they see the worm? Do they hear it?
Something in there must attract attention.
Inconceivable that the vessel itself
Could be so interesting, blood and lymph.
Men take to different vocations.
The sun burned, the grass was burned.
Each morning we woke to terror and hid our heads
Against the arrival of attendants.
Often the cry for help rose and was stifled
In our throats. At evening
Moths strove in hundreds against the screens.

The walls are of old brick, umber, tightly laid so that from
a little distance one sees no mortar; the roofs are of slate.

The windows are barred, but with grilles of curved ironwork
to look less forbidding.

On the grounds are many trees; I have seen hemlock, spruce,
white pine and scotch pine, white oak and red oak and
blackjack, sassafras, tulip, elm, swamp maple and Norway
maple, ironwood, birch, locust, shagbark hickory, apple
and plum, and willows in the distance.

Virginia creeper, the institutional vine, clambers the walls
and for a week in October looks like the longed-for fire.

Among the things which inmates are not permitted to possess
are: razors, knives, matches, bottles, jewelry (even wedding

rings are taken from those who wear them), cigarette lighters, tobacco cans, soap, or anything made from metal or glass.

Inmates must always ask for a light to be provided for their cigarettes, just as they must wait for a key to open every door; which makes for a great deal of business.

Inmates are prohibited from the use of the telephone, and all outgoing mail is read by the doctors.

The grounds, I am told, comprise 250 acres and include flower and kitchen gardens, an orchard, a golf course (for the staff), a pond (not in view).

The hospital is a large building with many wings which sprawls northward and southward for perhaps a quarter of a mile. It is divided between the Men's Side and the Women's Side.

Many other buildings lie scattered, like satellites: houses for doctors and administrative officials; apartments for residents and interns; dormitories for nurses and attendants; workshops; warehouses.

All told, four hundred inmates or thereabouts and seven hundred employees compose this community.

At first there are no visitors; later the doctors usually allow members of the family to visit between 2:00 and 5:00 on Mondays and Fridays.

Next to the rare occasions of genuine thought and feeling, the particulars, remote from a beautifying image, of a way of life are important; the incidental reflections are what we ought to do away with.

We rise at seven and go to bed at ten.

During the night there are inspections by the night-dwellers: we wake and jerk upright in the flashlight's glare.

We have English sparrows and pigeons and black crows. We have chipmunks and red squirrels and gray squirrels. I have seen doves and chicken hawks and rats and cockroaches. In the summer there were robins and once yellow finches.

One of the doctors, accompanied by the supervisor of nurses, makes an inspection round each morning and evening. At first the inmates greet the doctors with smiles, an attempt to seem cheerful and healthy; later they are sullen and silent and resentful; at last they are really exceedingly bored with the nuisance of these good mornings and good evenings.

To preserve themselves against this crowding misery, the nurses and attendants take up suffering too; never should I have thought to hear such squabbling and complaining among people who are selected explicitly for their evenness of temper.

The Men's Side is separated into wards called "halls": numbered Eight, Seven, Six, Five, Four and Two.

Hall Eight is for the murderous ones, the hall of packs and jackets to which attendants from other halls are sometimes curtly summoned.

Hall Seven is for "disturbed" folk, the hall of voices and shadows.

Hall Six is the convalescent ward, where those who have been shocked or worn into uniformity and submission—

I think some too achieve a certain understanding—wait and wait; intolerable waiting. Tempers are short on Hall Six, and often inmates are sent back to another hall.

Hall Five is the hall of the aged, the senile; it is the nursery in which those singular children play for a time before they fall back to the womb.

Hall Four is the admitting hall, where everyone goes first. Some remain there many months.

Hall Two is the "open" hall; inmates there are given the freedom of the grounds (during the day only and in a restricted area), and many receive "passes" on weekends.

There is an "Annex" too, somewhat mysterious. For the rhapsodists, the wolf people?

The Women's Side—the moon's other surface.

Poor poetry, true. But this is no proper writing room!

Pity not Ulysses, but the ear-stopped rowers.

The Shock Room is next to the Hydrotherapy Room.

Causes, effects—this their fusion, the Cartesian dénouement.

Each hall is equipped with a radio and a television set and about 25 inmates; some have pianos and billiard tables.

Chiefly this is the model of a despotism, disposed, one is assured, toward benevolent ends.

Many are committed here through the courts, and we have much talk of lawyers and writs and injunctions to restrain. We have many sea-lawyers.

13

The others commit themselves, so wretched are they.

"Hey, Gin-head! Twenty points for a pack of butts!"—
an invitation to billiards.

Aw, Dylan, have you left us? Have you gone?
An evil day it is. A day unblest.
My skin crept with the shiver of the air
This morning; it was a dark, reluctant dawn.
Another morning how the stars did stare
When our daft company jollified the west.
But Jim went south, and Harry's God knows where,
I'm in the booby hatch, and you are gone.

Aye, Dylan, tides there are to waft us all,
But you especially that blood and ink
Named for the sea: your christening was your call.
They say you died at St. Vincent's. Is it so?
I'd have sworn you perished in the bloody drink.
But deeper oceans flood the land; we know,
We crazy ones, how strong those waters flow.
If only you hadn't tried to drink it all.

And, Dylan, if the hills and woods of Wales
Still sound, as I've been told, with ancient song,
If winds there sputter Merlin's prophecies,
That is the land where Welshmen all belong.
It is an upland country, steep and strong,
Stemming a sea whose changing voice assails
The solitary heart. I think you please
To rest now in your song at home in Wales.

The year fell slowly.
The tilting planet sloped on its northward gyre
Languidly. Warm days lingered.
Indian summer was an endless converse
Among bored minds. I took the sun,
Its fierceness gone, trying its warmth
As old men test their baths,
And found it good. To bake one's bones
Is to ease the mysterious nerves.
On October afternoons, the morning fury over,
I lay on the lovely grass; the *plats*
Of tennis sounded distantly; crows cawed.
These were the hours of surcease, remembrances.
Sorrow and melancholy were a balm,
And I wrote a sonnet—

Of all disquiets sorrow is most serene.
Its intervals of soft humility
Are lenient; they intrude on our obscene
Debasements and our fury like a plea
For wisdom—guilt is always shared. The fears
Fall, if for just an hour, all away,
And the old essential person reappears.
Sorrow can shape us better than dismay.

You have forgiven me, old friends and lovers,
I think you have forgiven me at last,
As you put by the banished fugitive.
And if I'm sorry who was once aghast
For all the hurts I've done you, I forgive,
I too, the self this sorrow still recovers.

15

Indian summer, when sonnets are possible.
Yet so often sorrows are only
The flattery of regrets, and forgiveness
Is false and fond that flowers
From the perpetual garden of sentiment—the unforgivable
Stays, intrinsic to reality. All the rudenesses,
The steep blows that have been done
And are now ever and ever Hayden,
Oh they will not be drowned
In Melancholy's easy oblivion—
No Lethe till Styx is crossed!
(From *stygein*, to hate, fear.)
Reproach, reproach. Reality, the healthy prick!
"Ce n'est plus la vapeur qui produit la tonnerre,
C'est Jupiter armé pour affrayer la terre."
All sleeps, all dreaming, all day dreaming,
The dangerous hours; yet some slip through
And are gone, blissfully unaware,
Into oblivion. Even dread catatonia,
The frozen dream, may fall most softly
Upon a stony head: there terror strikes
Only in knowing one is struck.
The temptations of an October afternoon,
The soft, soft whispering of remembered love.

Another October we drove down from Salisbury
Among the Connecticut hills aflame with fall.
Blue sky and the frost sparkling, color
Of such depth and richness no Mediterranean
Day could hold it. I wish Matisse had seen it.
We stopped at The Three Oaks and had
Martinis before the fire; no one else was there.
Memories of Hartford and our night-long clinging.

Earlier Octobers, much earlier, I associate
With three arbors of concord grapes,

16

At Woodbury, at Briarcliff Manor, at Dover Furnace.
To wear a sweater, burn leaves, and eat grapes!

October passed as in a haze
Of burning. Pain cut a vivid course
Through these as through all days,
But hours of nothingness brought a low contentment;
Some of the shock of being wore away.
The year subsided, its seeming all aglow.

1

Ancient Mr. Barnes on Hall Five
possesses a body whose withness
                    in the Whiteheadian sense
surpasses all expectations
and certainly surpasses the
                    endurance of his mind.
Hence he is much jollity for the attendants.
But this morning:
        ATT. Hello, hello, Mr. Barnes. And who is
            president this morning?
        MR. B. Eisenhower, you goddamned fool!
'Sdeath!
        MR. B. And who's crazy now?
For once then not Mr. Barnes.
On another occasion
ancient Mr. Barnes
                    formerly a scholar
                    and I think a minister
was being conducted to the can
                    when he was overcome
                    by confusion.
        MR. B. Stop, stop, young man. What *is* it
            you want of me?

17

ATT. I want you to use the toilet, Mr. Barnes.

MR. B. What? What?

ATT. I want you to take a shit, Mr. Barnes.

MR. B. I shan't. I shan't shit.

Who's crazy now

*

In the morning we go to OT (Occupational Therapy) where
we weave belts from colored strings or work in the print-
shop or mess with clay and crayons. Our kindergarten.
Afterwards we go to Gym, where some play at basketball
or bowls or ping-pong.

In the afternoon the morning schedule is repeated.

Each inmate is assigned to one doctor, whom he sees more
or less once a week for more or less an hour.

The alcoholics, who sign on for a flat six months, see their
doctors less frequently.

The new attendant on Hall Six was fired yesterday for steal-
ing phenobarbital from the drug cabinet. A junky doing
his best.

The diet is a fattening one, purposely to make stout the starv-
ing drinkers and vomiters. Potatoes and gravy. Chicken and
rice. Pork and beans. The paranoiac at my table smells
his plateful, then asks me to exchange with him.

A melon and a pear, cheese and wine. (Bourceau and Chablis.)
My first lunch when I get out.

> The diagnosis is
> Anxiety psychoneurosis

(Chronic and acute)
Complicated by
Generalized phobic
Extensions and alcoholism.
Which is meaningless,
Even in clinical usage.
No doubt the files
Contain a description
In more precise language.
The fact is I am here,
Having collapsed, because
I can't be anywhere else—
The case with most of us.
And because the terrors
Which clutch and shake me,
The drink which wards them off,
Equally reduced me
To inaction, paralysis,
And extreme pain. I came
To the bin for the same
Essential reason anybody,
Injured in a fortuitous
Blast, goes to hospital. This
Place is supposed to help me.
But it's difficult, obtuse.
I may be walking in
Some placid sunny street,
Perfectly free and at ease,
Nonchalant you might say,
When the terror strikes—
Or rises or debouches or whatever.
It seizes me, whop!
Very fast. First, tension
In legs and neck, the flutter
Of hand to head; then

The general tremor, upheaval,
Sense of wobbling, falling;
Then panic, desperation.
To run, to fly, to sink—
To escape: an absolute command.
Fear of screaming, the sound
Bulging in the throat.
Heart-gasp and darkness
At the edge of the eyes.
Fear of fear. Terror is
Such a humiliating spectacle.
In busses, offices, theaters,
Shops, country roads and
Lonely woods, everywhere
But in beds and barrooms.

William James spoke
Of the experience and ascribed
It to an acute perception
Of evil—or some such;
I have no books. Yes,
Perception is involved,
A sharp sensory receptivity
To almost hidden things,
And evil of course is also
Involved, for you learn quickly
In fear nature's rapacities.
But it is more and less
Than that. More, because you
Track it down the fathering
Years as through a labyrinth
And encounter details,
So many inflowering
Centripetal courses of
Behavior, all related, all

Parts of a dreadful design
Which you can annotate
In terms of debasement and
Analyze in terms of cause
And effect. Less, because
You lose the powerful image,
The demon, the worm; you are
An ignoramus after all;
Worse, you are an ignoramus
Superior to James.

And the imbeciles who write
Biographies tell us now
It was all on account of
His father. At least our
Biographers won't have
The chance: we find out
For ourselves. And besides,
James Senior may
Have been the better man.
His father, the Albany puritan,
There was a real case!
Thence backward how far?
How far forward? The trials
Of the fathers are visited on . . .

The sons! Yes. Why can he
Never speak? The walls
Of the generations are higher,
Thicker than these walls.
Silence. But the fathers
Pay too, and pay and pay.

Well, the causes of any
Personality make dull

Reading, all the queasy
Toils and complaints, jounces
Of any particular fate.
Ask any bartender.
Why should the shop talk
Of psychiatrists engage
An era's attention? Let
The filth of the studious
Seances lie hidden; let it
Age in the hospital records;
Let it be burned someday
With all the rest.

                    But
Some events are humanly
Sharable.

          The first
Is the momentous seizure,
The bolt that flings one
Into separateness and
Establishes the disability.
Until then one is never
Alone, but afterwards
One cannot even shriek
Across the distances, for none
Can hear—friends, lovers,
Blood relations. Oh,
Alas! It's true, self-knowledge
Comes to everybody, but not
With our murdering rush,
The brain's explosion.
Then doubts burst in like
Floodwater and all is lost
In wreckage. One swirls away.

The land moves, leaving
Nothing to grasp. To be going,
Slipping, sprawling, wallowing,
Sinking—that is the panic.
To wish to be gone is the
Temptation, the only hope.
Once I wrote a poem,
A recitative I called it
Deceptively, to catch that hour.

oris Cerberei spumas et virus Echidnae
erroresque vagos caecaeque oblivia mentis
et scelus et lacrimas rabiemque et caedis amorem

(From Ovid, the epigraph
Deceptive too, as if I had
More than small Latin.)

Outlandish ribbons did not rake the sky
With rosiness; no quake
Beyond the admonitions of my blood
Convulsed the air; a blackbird failed to cry;
The cool and mirroring lake
Gave no pretense of spume or scud
To grieve an omen-seeking eye.
At first the recollection of the past I sought—
Walking the lakeshore, far from any flood
Of loosening clamor in the nerve—
Obscured the feathered rustlings, the awake
And nesting ones, wings of reserve
Amid the leaves of temper trembling like a lie.
The lake was nothing but an April's thought.

Who conjured heaven from the children's world?
There were the sweet remembrances of gleams

From a golden cutlass whirled
Like a din of glee among the peonies,
The day's first sky, a trout beside a crow,
The veiling curve
Of a birch-hemmed path to a hidden place of dreams,
And of course the winsome virtue of the snow.
Again, swept by the seize
Of oceanic memory in the mind,
I sensed the soft
Insistence of an actual rock
Without a shock.
No thought divined
The source of strength that held me so, aloft.
Yet on the safe lakeshore
Where memory roamed in lovely *ands* and *whethers*
Terrors unknown before
Burst from the hard conjunction of new words
Like a flight of stars loosed from their aerial tethers.
At memory's accident the unsaid pains
Gossiped like an elm of frightened birds.
All nerves were wings. The rains
Of memory hissed in the mind's quick fires.
What thuds against the hollow ears!
A cry to murder is a trumpet call,
The boy's voice crying down the fathering years.

Now buzzing stars bedizen distant spires,
And in the center where the waters brawl
With a thousand fishes, silvery as coins,
The sick gull rides the rising pedestal.
His musty feathers effuse his rotten flesh.
His eye is sealed by a membranous lid.
His beak is parting, bursting, and it joins
On a swollen tongue. And still the fishes thresh
The water like strewn money; still the cloud

Trundles the sky as if it were a squid.
The gull will fall! O gull, then you will fall!
(At no time say these words aloud.)
He falls, head down, like a stone,
Swift as an eagle's pearly lees, the invalid,
To the fishes. Listen, the birds intone
A sigh of wings that settles like a shroud.
Mother of warning, what has now occurred?
Shall I reach out a hand? Am I too proud?
Quick, quick! Pull back. Don't touch the dirty bird.

       That was Chicago, a happening
       By the lake, baroque—
       So friends informed me—florid,
       Nonsensical, abstruse.
       I had a private triumph,
       Nothing more. But it
       Was fully that, and still
       These three years later my words
       Seem exact as algebra.
       But no, I'd not condone
       Such an affront to mind
       As the response to this poem
       Seems to make it, yet
       I'm loath to give it up.
       It's of me too much, it's
       My own knowing, and it makes
       Me shudder if no one else
       Turns a hair. Tell me, what
       Do you know of Pillicock-hill
       Anyway? Has it occurred
       To your eminences
       That the grips of lunes are not
       Fit emprize for pavid
       Imaginations? We, we are

The ones hardened and rudely
Enriched by these trials,
For all our weaknesses that you
Delight on, and, it may be,
Made braver, forced to endure.

But I should not anger. The seizures
Came then oftener and
Oftener, until all my hours
Were a span of anxiety,
A life grotesque. Once
When I was teaching at
A small college in Gary,
Indiana, I ran from the
Classroom, fleeing wildly,
Leaving everything, and I ran
To the Gary station and caught
A train to Chicago. I
Never went back. For all
I know those earnest, pretty
Boys and girls may still
Be sitting there, waiting.

I was able to take only
Five minutes of *The Medium.*

Busses and trains were unbearable,
And voices in large rooms.

Now as I write the memory
Starts up again the scramble
In my brain, the drive of blood.

The psychiatrists took up
The case in two cities

And during seven years;
Contending methodologies
Harassed me on that berme,
The deepnesses before me.
A behaviorist did his
Futile best (six months
And I don't remember how
Many dollars), but chiefly
Psychoanalysis engaged me,
The infuriating science
Of silence and bewilderment.
I am crazy, I am not,
I said, plucking the daisy
Petals of my anxiety:
I am a murderer, I am a
Corpse, a lecher or a prude,
A fish or a fowl or a teddy
Bear—wellaway!
The story is a modern
Commonplace and can be
Found in many of the more lurid
Documents of the age.
The point is, though it took
Me years to see it, the theories
All come to the same end,
All are views of the same
Disaster, which was also seen
Previously by such diverse
Observers as Marcus Aurelius,
Rabelais, and Miss Austen.
Meanwhile anxiety stayed,
The ocean did not run dry.

To dig at Luxor, to peer
At the sky from Mount Wilson,

To hunch in Paris over
A Sumerian fragment or in
Princeton over the eternal
Deceptions of measurement—
These are the occupations
Of men I admire and envy.
These are the dreams in which
Men lose themselves, the dreams
Of objectivity. Vanity
Becomes so needful to them
That no one calls them vain,
And they themselves think
To add something to the cubits
Of the world. Fascinating
And in no way criminal,
That mode of life, and weakness
Asks no more.

Herodotus
Saw farther than most without
Really looking very hard.
It's what one wants that counts.

I don't mean to say
There weren't good times.
The bad predominated.
Booze helped immensely.
Work also, but not,
Unfortunately, writing.
Friends and parties and lovers
Lent ease to my unease
Sparingly. The doctors kept
The anxious pot aboil.
So passed the years.

When I say they were filled
With disaster I am not
Joking, not by a damn sight:
Tragedy hasn't gone from
Our lives, even if the meanness
Of the cultural environment
Prevents us from believing it.
The disasters were seen by many,
The consequences are palpable.
Time healed nothing,
Nor has it ever, though death
Has. The two are not to be
Confused. The years passed.
After the hurts, the fears.
After the fears, the escapes.
After the escapes, the despairs.
My solicitous friend, Dr. Gin,
Came often to my house.
The house closed in; I,
My cat, and my poor girl
Watched the world gibber
And clung to the tilting floor.
The birds swam dreamily
Past the windows, and somewhere
A siren wailed incessantly.
The city was enormous,
And our cell broken down and
Unnoticed in all the wreckage.
But at last a dear lady
Of mercy came to help me.

And I found myself here
In the hot time of the year.

Many of my friends who are poets
and who have set themselves up to hold views
have construed recent intellectual history
as a phase of withdrawal and disdain:
their custom is to decry
civilization
and as a convenient collapsible image of it
they have hit on the cocktail party
Their opinion has currency and perhaps
                    an element of justice

But let me use the occasion
to point out that no civilization
has been much good
                goodness being an end to which men
                in a condition of statehood do not aspire
and to affirm my own belief
that cocktail parties
                are not only salutary
                but damn near indispensable
People who attend them to drink highballs
        or other dilutions
are rejecting their own civic responsibilities
and acting in bad taste:
                cocktail parties are for the
                consumption of martinis
In an age of specializations
and antipathies
the cocktail party is a necessary
instrument of concord
and close to a real anarchic commune
I have always enjoyed myself at cocktail parties
I have found many friends there

30

I have never done anything altogether impure
              or ignoble at a cocktail party
and I have said many honest things
I have got as close as I expect I ever shall
              in other words
              to wisdom
and the real problem may be not how to
get rid of cocktail parties
              but how to prolong them

      Am I serious?
          I don't know
      I don't know my own mind
      What is seriousness
          when everything is so goddamned important?

                    1

December now. Winter deepens and darkens. Stars
Shine distantly in the trees when we return
From Gym at five o'clock, reminding us,
Not of our smallness—only abstractions are large—
But of our loneliness on this lost planet.
And in the morning hoarfrost lies on the hemlocks,
And white rime glitters on my window's bars.
The winds roam endlessly among our wings and ells,
Massive old choirs singing their desolation.
Within, the drafts play coldly through our halls.
I write in my small cell at a table placed
Before the window, the only space I have,
And my hands are stiff with cold. Mongolia where
These winds originate seems bleak and hostile.

Thin snow sifts on the hard pavement there,
Stone buildings rise like towers of ice.

Bitter, bitter blows the wind in those streets,
Freezing poor faces like anesthesia,
Blinding poor eyes with winter's tears. I see
The girls with thin-clad legs and hunched shoulders
Who scurry and jitter and tremble and stand and weep:
How unlovely they are, all bleary and pinched.
I think of their clay-cold breasts and their blue knees.
The men too, with drops at the ends of their noses—
Their hands hurt, as if they were made of money.

The age of wonders. Who would have thought the dream
Of luxury could live in these freezing heads?

What shall I say? What shall I do?
That place I call Mongolia is home.
There I was born, there I remained for more
Than thirty years, not different from the others.
I also walked those freezing streets, and the cold
Sank in my skull and swished against my ankles.
I found sometimes a curious joy in knowing
The pain of life, in being one of the many
Who tinkled grimly down the cold steps to hell
On the Lexington Avenue line.

And sometimes there was joy unmodified,
An hour stolen, a noon
When trees and clouds fortuitously shaped
Contentment. Other joys, more livid, pressed
Minutes and hours into the plastic evenings.
I saw and considered and I judged
As others did, and if I knew more fear
Than they, I called it my inheritance
And said the world is as it must be. I
Was even readier than some to yield

The image of happiness. I thought, then, this
Is possible, this world, if one has courage.

The bitcheries of Madison Avenue
Where I lost my mind, where pigs that learned to read
Talk moneywise around the urn of love;
The stink of certain senators that reaches,
As in Chicago every nose perceives
The stockyards on a foggy day, across
The country, fouling every wind; the creamy
Excrement of Hollywood; the noise
Which fulsome sentiment emits in moans
And wailings—falsely imitating war—
Wherever our sick young assemble; the goads
And insults of the advertising writers;
The insipidities of bread and beer
And all the goods of this commercial era;
The slattern minds that waste away the schools
And foul the house of thought with personal lust—
The catalogue of our misfortunes, oh
How long it is, so have the false men prospered!
Yet for the sight of red-winged blackbirds in
The spring, and for their song, and for
The sight and song of love, I kept at home
And said Mongolia was my proper country.

But having lost that country I look back
With loathing deeper than ever I thought to feel.

I see that country in the winter skies
Reflected from beyond the wall. The stars,
So distant and faint, signify a space
More vast than I can understand, but empty,
In no way tempting, cold, impersonal.
Up there I see no image of myself,

But chaos, furious and dull. Beyond
The roof, beyond the wall, the spaces stretch
Away to nothingness, and here and there
A cold light moves. I hear the wind. But now
I seldom see the shadows hurrying there.

1

I have done a small survey, like any good Frobenius, on the present inhabitants of Hall Six.

We are 24 inmates all told.

The oldest is 76 years of age, the youngest is 19.

The one who has served the longest time in the hatch has been here thirteen years. The shortest is six weeks.

Four are repeaters; that is, this is their second sentence in this hatch. Three others were previously in other hatches.

Sixteen have had electroshock therapy.

Twelve are from New York; five from New Jersey, two from Connecticut, and one each from Kentucky, Texas, New Mexico, Alabama and England.

There are two Catholics, six Jews, ten Protestants, and five agnostics.

Unanimity of belief exists on only one proposition: man's chief joy is fornication.

The 24 inmates may be classified as follows:

    1 accountant
    2 salesmen
    1 musician

3 businessmen (grocer, hotelkeeper, corporation executive)
1 priest
1 advertising copywriter
1 merchant marine
5 college students
1 playboy
4 doctors
1 taxi driver
1 airplane mechanic
1 gambler
1 radio announcer

They may be further classified as follow:

7 manic-depressive psychoses
        (2 manic types, 3 depressive, 2 circular)
7 schizophrenia (1 simple, 1 catatonic, 5 paranoid)
1 psychasthenia
2 anxiety psychoneuroses
6 alcoholics
1 drug addict

Note: most inmates believe the alcoholics have the easiest portion; neither their illness nor their treatment seems particularly uncomfortable, even though the percentage of permanent cures is low—a little sodium amytal and some vitamin shots during the first days in the hatch are usually enough to straighten them out. The alcoholics themselves believe this and hold themselves somewhat aloof from the rest of us, who are crazy.

1

Policemen in Mongolia laugh and sneer.
They walk among realities all day.

35

Their passion is to utter common sense.
Sweet reason abides with them, they always know
An answer. "Hek," they say, and "Hek-a-hek!"
Such laughter sounds with the strident horns and bells.
The trusses truss, the pulleys pull. The cops
Who always have an answer know this well.
And what if they are right? Oh, what of that?
The shadowy gentleman also laughs and sneers.
He knows, he knows. Therefore what can be said?

The mark of Darius was a crescent moon,
A token chipped in very ancient stone.

When Hector fell his blood thrice stained the field,
And thrice a wail ascended from the wall.

A certain captain sped the other day
At twice the speed of sound across the sky.

In a closed room, sealed tight against the world,
I should eventually suffocate.

A fourteenth way: the blackbird plummets down,
Severing the snowy world with his death-fall.

Ah many, many are the ways of numbers;
I am astounded by their roots and powers.

These things have excellence occasionally:
Fire hydrants, universities, trombones.

And these are excellent intrinsically:
A burning candle, a family, a guitar.

But these have excellence only in an eye:
A fiery cross, a flight of ducks, a singing wife.

Thus aspects of reality unfold
Over us like the clouds or like a rain
That makes a stunning humdrum for our ears.
And we can name the truths that built the world,
And we can laugh when the policeman laughs.
The shadowy gentleman who walks the fields
With explanations handy for all things,
Shall I not join him in his scorn for me?
He is responsible. Let him laugh if he can!
The world of fears and dreams is not a world;
It is not place, not country, not a time.
Hammer and nails will build a house for me,
Wood for the rafters, plaster for the walls,
And a maple tree to shade me in the summer—
The objects belonging in Mongolia.
To make a shadow one must stand in the sun,
Is it not so? Yes, laughter is the speech
Of reality, telling us to touch,
To kick out like Sam Johnson and achieve
A sudden entrance to the solid world.
Why all the searching? Why the puzzlement?
Idiot. Have you lost your way so soon?
You've walked that journey a thousand times before!
But I hear an ancient wail of blood—

Save me, O God; for the waters are come in
          unto my soul.

I sink in deep mire, where there is no standing:
I am come into deep waters, where the floods
          overflow me.

I am weary of my crying: my throat is dried:
          mine eyes fail . . .

37

Deliver me out of the mire, and let me not sink:
let me be delivered from them that hate me,
    and out of the deep waters.

Let not the waterflood overflow me, neither
        let the deep swallow me up,
        and let not the pit
        shut her mouth upon me.

The feminine flood from Palestine's faint hills
Still sings to us down the coiling centuries,
A lisping of the sea that lies within.
Magnificent waters, spacious coasts, and winds
Dipping and glimmering like a jewel, all caught
In this little compass. Never do the waves
Cease running like a whisper on those shores,
Reminding us of danger; languid tides
Slope there forever, rounding endlessly,
And beware the turn to storm, for then the sea
Rages in its small scope most dreadfully.
Waves surge and burst, white foam springs away,
Winds hurl the water wantonly and wrack
The coasts. The howl and thunder sounding there
Can drench our ears, the seas can drown our nerves.
It is the storming time when we are broken.
Anciently the psalmist mourned that sea
For all of us; his drowning heart called out
For all of us; and we still hear the call,
A misery that rises in our throats.
This sea that drowns us, does it sweep away
The trees and houses of reality?
Shall we at last forsake the gentleman
Who bids us look and see the trees and houses?
For I know well what happened on my walk
To make the thousand times I'd walked before

No better than the useless memory
Of how to tell the time or tie my shoes.
Reality itself was useless then,
At least in its old semblance. If I walked
Where I had walked before but found a sea
Spilling and lapping among the trees and houses
Could I expect to pass through safe and dry?
The flood became a new reality,
Tritoned and serpented of course, a world
By virtue of its sweeping me away.
I don't deny a captor that decisive.
The plunge from certainty to mystery,
From reason to wild wondering, is deep
And dangerous, like any exploration.
New knowledge, like the turbulence of sex,
Breaks on us, whirling, sending us down, creating
A maelstrom of all familiar things. We see
Stigmata bloom upon our usual flesh.
Polaris fades among the many stars.
Hysteria is common, but so cruel!
Only the mothers find ripe easement then,
Making in their unwilled but sensitive bodies
An integration of reality.
The rest are saints and poets, gibbeted
For love to peck at and for hate to freeze.
No revelation in the desert speaks,
But only a way to die, or a way to work.
And when the trees and houses tumble down
We find the real remnant in memory
And sometimes in foresight; but we know
Reality will never be safe again,
Nor any image made to a fixed design.
We fear the honest more, the knavish less;
In noiseless dreams we suffer at world's end;
We see especially the darkness of

The little passage down the days and weeks;
And all the blindness and the ranting there,
The way of the world, is our despair and torture;
The touch of money turns us stark and sick;
We know the hand that withers in the fire,
The burned heart, and the fearfulness of love.

1

Conversation at billiards:
Hey, Gin-head! Twenty points for a pack of butts?
O.K. But no filters, and all scratches count.
You break.
You.
We'll shoot for it. Loser breaks.
Oya! Look at this cue, crookeder than a cat's ass!
Same as this.
Wouldn't you think they'd spend a buck?
                              These are for firewood.
Shoot and quit yapping.
Jesus, what a lousy shot.
A set-up.
Yeah? If you could draw that you'd be a billiard player.
Shoot.
Kiss, you bastards, kiss!
Ow, what luck.
Rack me up a point, boy.
You couldn't make this in a hundred years.
A rough one, too thin. I'll follow it.
Shoot.
Aw, the table slants.
It slants the other way, lush. You're a yard off.
Shoot.
Wha! La scratche!
I owe one.

40

You're damn right. Give up?
Etc., etc.

The rule of the majority is
strictly enforced in all matters
concerning the television set.
Whereas one might suppose that
we should look at "Suspense"
nine times and something else
once, in fact we see "Suspense"
ten times—those who can bear
to see it. The sound reaches
to the farthest cell. No less
than sedition to suggest that
the damn thing be turned off.

Listen, fossils, the faucet
drips other distractive meters.
Could a wrench stop tears?
I'd tighten my eyeballs
sideways. But everywhere
white dominates, like hate
in a quiet woman full of waiting.

Prizefight. Heavyweight
championship. We are permitted
to stay up past curfew, a special
occasion. Dark room, spectral
light. How tension grips me,
violence without and within.
Heart hammers, heaves. Images
flare in a gust of light.
Long before knockout I retreat
and lie in my cell in the dark,
hidden, trembling, the loser.

Political discourse:
Oh well, southern Democrats—that's a horse of another color.
 I like southern Democrats all right.
Not another dime! No sir, why should we support Europe?
They're the ones that start all the wars anyways.
Let me tell you, this country will never be right as long as the
 labor unions control the government!

From my window a crow cawing.
Each time he flaps his wings.

The lay psychiatrists:
A bunch of punks, that's what. What do they care? I never
 saw such doctors.
The suckers. How come they let Mercer out so soon?
He's here before. Second time is quicker.
Yeah, how about Drisco? Two years he's here the second time.
What do you expect? He slugged his old lady. If he goes out
 they stick him in jail.
Aw, he's wackier than a three-legged duck anyway.
Yeah, how about you? At least he ain't got no scars on his
 wrists.
Look what's talking. You piss out the window every night.
What the hell is this dementi preecock anyhow?
It's a jail, that's what it is. A goddamn jail.
I ain't even seen a doctor in three weeks. And I'm supposed
 to get well in this joint?
Three weeks? You're lucky. I ain't seen mine in six.
But you're in on an alky rap.
Yeah, they're going to send me downtown to a AA meeting
 next week. Can you figure that? Why didn't they do it six
 months ago if that's the best they can offer?
Knock it off, knock it off. Here comes the doctor.

"The free evening fades, outside the windows fastened with
 decorative iron grilles."

Lights blare, trumpeting into the safe dark corners.
The billiard players assemble; the bridge players cut for
partners.
In the corner television sets up its obscure ruckus.
Fear moderates, now day's demands are gone. The haze of
tobacco smoke is reassuring.

The reader finds new intentness in his marveling;
The astonishing peace of his confidence, at first so faint is
renewed:
Beauty is not fierce after all.
He looks up and around; he thinks: these people are busy
without me.

Contentment surrounds the quiet talkers
Who are deft with their cigars; already the people they were,
Choking and screaming, are forgotten; they have become old
men, their sex only legendary.
That one's habitual gesture, when he presses his fingertips to
his temples, does not even remind him.
They do not notice the bell that taps so insistently for one of
the doctors.

Slowly and calmly the children have been murdered and
buried.
Nightmares have been put away, dusty storybooks.
Love's ecstasy has been left in the country of the unreal.

Is this the evening for Mr. W to trip down the hall
On his toes, teetering like a top, his tongue stiffened with fear?
Mr. B looks obliquely through the window at the red and
yellow lights in the valley.

1

All night the snow hissed against my window.
Now the whorls of the grille bear half-circles

43

of snow, crescent and decrescent.
Beyond, the maples and oaks are traceries
        of white
and the firs are downy. I long
to say with the lazy poets
        and young lovers
Winter has wrought this faerie. But
in winter our orbit only rises, nor can
we say our lord sun has departed.

Urbi et orbi
and this is no bull.

Boreas, the hoarfrost and the snow
are taken from you. Jack cannot paint
my window any longer. These crystals
and condensations fall upon us
        from the sky's inglorious machine
and if beauty be with us for a morning
we give thanks to fortuitous vapors,
        for here is no creation.

To the city and to the world
poets are liars
painters are prestidigitators
sculptors are sleight-of-hand performers
        and philosophers are bitter men.

Yet Boreas I'll find a use for you. You were
        ever a dreamer
        never a maker.
Only foolish poets and painters and sculptors
strive with the lifeless elements
        and philosophers are best let alone.
        You were

44

content to see in the blind snow, to dream.
You dreamed the transmutations of the night,
a melting dream that leaves us when we tire
          and leaves us the bare world.
We are the lost ones Boreas who love
          insubstantial things—
the white swift tree of summer when storm turns up the leaves
the haze of poppies on an Italian hill
the oracle a wind speaks in the pines
the devastation of a cloud's shadow
and now the dazzling of the snow.

Once on a night in spring
                    I remember
I sat at the end of the long curving jetty
whose base is attached to the city of Chicago—
that is to say, it bends into Lake Michigan
          from North Avenue.
I had turned my back to the city
          and I watched the stars.
It was a night to think of poems to write.
Then, weary of poems, I sprawled back
letting my head hang upsidedown from the pier.
I looked toward Chicago; the lake was above me.
In the watery sky the city shone and glimmered.
Up, up it reached, tower on tower, into
          the black depths
where fishes with alien intelligence kept
          motionless company.
And earth below me was strewn with stars.
Oh it was a dancing delicate rippling world,
     so bright, gaiety beyond noise and laughter,
in the water of all souls' drowning.
Deeply it rose, darkly it shone, and I drew
breaths of cool water, coming alive in that world.

But, magnificently, a fish jumped, and the city
flew apart, sparks in the wind,
       and only the stars were still.

The snow country rolls and dips, and the fields gleam.
The trees are frozen plumes, icicles fringe the eaves.
The black crow moves across the snow,
making the world spin. Round goes the world,
we all spin, dizzy and snow-blind, crazy
as drunken elves. Oh the brittle world,
won't it break—spears and daggers and all?
It's broken, it's broken.

      My lady of snow
      you are a young girl
      who laughs.
                Wive me, marry me!
      Come let's fall in
      the snowdrift. We're warm.
      Care nothing for frost.
      We're merry. Such wine
      did we drink that winter.
      Ho love, we are gliding,
      I am the faster.
      Catch me, kiss me.
      Oh God, are your legs broken?

      Oh God, are her legs broken?

To the monastery and to Mongolia
please do not misunderstand me
my heart is heavy and burdened with sorrow
these are the days of peril
I would come to you with my love
      with my hands and my lips

no one touches me and no one calls
I say to you please forsake your ways
        and your looking, your searching
remember me in these messages of anguish
remember how much I have loved you
        and how I have tried to help you

Snow. Reality is no more. Appearance
is the measure of my love. I see the snow
drifting beyond this warm, red room
where the leopard sleeps before the fire.

Urbi et orbi
these are the messages of a winter

In the snowy courtyard
        someone has strung lights
            red and blue

on the little fir and we have a holly wreath
        in the window at the end
            of the hall.

The dim Judean hills lie beyond the wall
        and a star shines at the corner
            in the top of my window.

In these fantastic halls an ancient love
        floats like a wisp of time
            on this strange Christmas.

1

All, all of a piece throughout!
Thy Chase had a Beast in View;
Thy Wars brought nothing about;

Thy Lovers were all untrue.
'Tis well an Old Age is out
And time to begin a New.

1

The scene is laid, the problem ascertained;
The culprit stands up bravely, self-arraigned.

The cross-examination must begin
To find how far his guilt is genuine.

This is the court where men are self-confessed;
The unknown crime is what we must contest.

He stands his own accusor, and the trial
Is called to prove the jury's sly denial.

It is a curious court. The smug defense
Is prodded by the judge from indolence.

The judge himself is known to tell a lie,
To man the ways of man to justify.

The jurymen are worthy and untrue;
All good brass monkeys know what not to do.

Guilt is rewarded with imprisonment;
Freedom is sentenced on the innocent.

No witnesses are called; the prisoner's word
Is credited for all that has occurred.

And he both testifies and sits above
To look down on the testing of his love.

Make no mistake, his love is what we try,
Though he will sneer and turn away his eye.

The measure of that love we shall obtain:
The need, the doubt, the scruple, and the pain.

And therein we shall find at last the cause,
Not of his breach, but of the very laws.

The court assembles on this New Year's Day.
The case, I fear, will stretch far, far away.

Many adjournments, many dull vexations
Will interrupt our course and try our patience.

And sometimes, when the court commits a gaffe,
We may enjoin the prisoner to laugh.

All this in roughly metric paraphrase
Will be adduced in these communiqués

The better to coerce a living fear
Toward order in this critical new year.

But any trial is a small affair.
To meet the general terror is our prayer,

To know the mercy we must mete to him
Who hurts himself, to ease the interim

Of anger, and to share his dark distrust;
These are the obligations of the just.

In such a practice we who have been hurled
Aside may learn once more the joyous world.

Expectantly and fearfully I sing.
A bird must walk that has a broken wing.

1

The chain screams in the hawsehole, the anchor plunges.
Bubbles stream from the flukes, making deep augury.
Is there landhold at this anchorage?

This is the andantino.

"O speak no more of love and death
And speak no more of sorrow:
My anger's eaten up my pride
And both shall die tomorrow."

To voyage again, outward again—
No, that were jeopardy.
Sink here, encaged here.
Build here an iron ship,
A calendar of iron days.

A steely will to keep out fear,
An iron heart to keep out love,
And poets may create themselves.

This is safe anchorage
And this is an iron ship;
The treacherous currents sweep yonder,
The storms rage outside, and the wide
Blue sea dips and winks in sunlight;
These are the memories of sea, the images
That will not disappear
Even in this safe anchorage here.

Today is still a day of choice,
The anchor is not fast.

Swift as desire, a tern flashes—
Out to sea, out to sea!

My past is like a tern flying.
It swoops insolently under my eyes,
Then is a speck lost on the horizon.

Lost. Loss. The melancholy bell.

Lost sweetheart, how our memories creep
Like chidden hounds, and come to reap
All fawningly their servient due,
Their tax of pity and of rue,
So that my hope of sanity
Like sternness dies and falls from me.
The day I build with plotted hours
To stand apart is mine, not ours.
Its joyless business is my cure;
Stern and alone, I may endure.
But memory though it slumber wakes
And deep in the mind its havoc makes.
A distant baying reels and swells
And floods the night, and so dispels
My hardness; hours dissolve and fall;
My loss is double, you then all.
Dearest, are you so unaware:
For here, in mine, your senses share
These broken hours and tumbled days
That are no longer mine. Your ways,
The body's blossoms, breast and eye,
The soft songs of your hands, the shy
And quick amusement of your smile—
My constant losses, these beguile
All my new bravery away.
If you have gone, why do you stay?

51

If here, then why have we no ease?
Loss is a blindness that still sees,
A handless love that touches still.
Loss is a ravage of the will.
And the incontinence of loss,
Mad loneliness, turns all to dross,
Love to a raging discontent
And self to a shabby tenement.
The mind is hapless, torn by dreams
Where all becoming only seems
A false impossible return
To a world I labor to unlearn.

In the fog this January
Comes the sound of little soft waves
Lapping against the rusty hull
And the sound of the terns crying.
Behind the fog is the great sea.
Swiftly my losses come to me.

Swiftly we have fled. Already it is
A new age, and only twenty years
Have made the difference. Then
Cooper and Scott were a boy's books,
And in the deep countryside
There were no mechanical ideas.
Rock and river and snow,
The fields and the forests
Were our secure neighborhood.
In that world we made our sport
And became wise early, knowing
The ways of lichen and toad.
In the forests we learned
Love from the foxes and owls
And from a girl.

The woods
Were filled with snow and bright
Under the winter moon, a new country
Of strange shapes and shadows.
Thunder roamed under the deep ice
Of the pond, driven by the cold
Against the banks, and we left
And walked back through the trees,
Our hands together, our skates
Clinking in the silence.

Girl of long ago,
Ours is the longest separation,
Our love is love's perpetuation.

Children in the snow,
For love we gave our loss most dearly,
Knowing the safe years gone obscurely.

Our quick portentous touch
Spoke more than we had ever spoken
And told us we were made and broken.

We were never such
As quickly conquer love's distresses;
Shyly our doubts engaged our guesses.

And yet our time of joy,
That moment of unity, created
The image life has imitated.

It was an ardent boy
Who loved you, Marjorie, and even
Now he knows the love you've given.

Among all these nameless and these falsely named
Let this name stand true: Marjorie Marie St. Pierre,

The unforgettable. We were in fact thirteen years old,
But some leap to hotness sooner than others, especially
In a farming community. It was an exploration of innocence,
A searching into all our imaginings of beauty, an unexpected
Vision of our own loveliness, which we acknowledged
    delightedly.
And we were fourteen and then fifteen, and then the sword
Cleaved. A swift clean stroke, the world fell in two.
The elders were responsible, or perhaps a distant word.
I began my disconsolate wandering on the burned plain,
And the forests of snow, the green fields became
My Eden. The first loss, incommensurable. Afterwards
Many toils, many fantasies interposed a real world.
I wonder how my Marjorie fared these twenty years.
Love's faintest gesture would be to say good luck.
Too faint. Our hazards, our chances destroy us, but
I'll wish her wisdom to choose before luck.

                                        A perfect stone
Of goodliness weighs in my mind, weathering
All the erosions that cut and wash away the soft
Groves of nerves, the silts of idleness and accident
And a thousand and one mornings. I carry it,
A treasure, everywhere, my balancing stone, my precious stone.
It is a smooth and intricate design, shaped
To a living girl, yet changeless and worn hard
By the watery or sandy winds that circulate
Through my veins. It curls inside my skull, an embrace
Close to the bone, enclosing deathlessly in stone
The only faithfulness that has endured, uninjured.
Such a companion did I pray for when I began
My journeying on the burned plain, my crouching
In the wider crater that has become my home.
And when it was given to me, a rude gift to hurt me,
I was not hurt, but thankful and pleased to possess something.

54

I worked with my shaping hands, molding and caressing,
To make a beautiful stone, and it has grown ever
More in grace and love, my image, my stone, my girl
Who makes me and shapes me as I turn her form
In my hands; I am the partner of the stone.
The gift that came to me from the heaven of disdain
Is my saint, my protectress, the only faith I have kept
When all the other images shattered on their screen
Like broken shadows and disintegrated in the smoke.
My monument I rescued from that other country
And brought to the burned plain, the eyeless crater.
When the fiery sun danced on the horizon, twirling
And bending in seductive sensuous gleams, I ran
Often, calling, imploring for such golden loves and truths,
But always fell, face in the sharp grass, weeping,
Until the comfort of my stone restored me, saying,
"To be true." I knew, I knew. Dancing suns
All come to this. My true stone, I was true to you,
Though I broke all the others. And one day, far
On the burned plain, the clouds in the fierce sky
Flew, and their shadows on the plain flew, and I turned fast
To find my way, but confused voices betrayed me,
Far on the burned plain. I ran that way, that way, that way,
Like three men. And the sudden dark descended with a crash.
I awoke here, with my true stone, in this graveyard
Where other journeyers have come too, bringing their stones.
Many stones are here, all true, all old and beautiful.
The savage methodical men
                              go among them with heavy hammers.

That was the lyric way, touched, one knows, by sentiment,
But also the limpid, honeyed by the truth that abides in
The geometries of the past, the clear configurations that we
See when years run together. People once were likely to
Perceive in their remembrances the ungual gentleman

At work, so dire and ineluctable are time's
Disclosures, and though the fashion in such matters has
Somewhat altered, our methods and our madnesses are
Much of the same old piece. Not to be wondered at or
Cried over, at least not for an appreciable moment. The
Telling of the human condition, which has so long
Occupied the artificers of "naturalism," I cannot call
A sufficient warrant for the poet's inevitable presumptions.
I'd say again my study is to be ironical. I expound a cause
Which I have seen on thousands of faces, my eye of course
Having been somewhat better trained than most for
The observation of distress. Hence the melic mode is
Questionable, though its effective reinforcement of the
Primary content is a useful device. We are liars and
Dreamers and beautifiers and dramatizers, but we are
Also courageous in the need to destroy our products, to
Cut through the wish of words to the past in its wholeness.
Plains and Edens are O.K. *after* the scrutator has
Established the incorruptibility of his wretched scruples.

There were other forests then—not so many as to
Enrapture a maiden's secret hours, but enough to
Deepen the experience of loss.

                              North Carolina where the day
Is always afternoon, where smoke from the cabins
Of the first settlers still hangs in the air and the
Speech of those same gentle folk sounds in the clearings.
A tall forest there, with pine trees rising like pillars
Straight and high. These were the ancient trees, making
A cathedral of the earth, shadowed and quiet, carpeted
With soft needles. A ray of sunlight broke through
The foliage and slanted into the gloom
As from a high window, lighting a broad stump that
Might have been an altar for our rites. We wandered there,

56

While war broke on the nations. Images of death,
Real soldiers leaping from bullet-bites in the news reels,
Made us unsurprised at our sudden adulthood, and fear
Made love in that cathedral more urgent and beautiful
Than ever anywhere. Then we became soldiers and
Took up our dying.

　　　　　　In Illinois, where the woods are
Like Christmas with bright haws and the white
Birches, we walked, momentarily free from the
Stern punishments of anxiety, or in the spring among
The enchanted avenues of the crabapples in full bloom.

Chicago, the Appalachian city, rustic, worn, and dirty,
Edges close to the lake, the jewel, and we walked
The shore, watching the endless changes of color and shape
In the water.

　　　　　　Wisconsin in mid-summer was bright green,
The exclamation of green, and of growth, of fertility,
Of love.

　　　　　　Being people, we sought our kind in the city,
And our love claimed its life in the roach-infested
Tenements, strayed drunkenly to the parks, spurred us
To ravishment at parties, to the terrible itch of our touch
At theaters; we thieved.

　　　　　　New York means ecstasy
In rain, the closeness of churchlike cocktail lounges,
Walking in endless rain at the Battery, West Fourth Street,
Third Avenue under the El, Thirty-Seventh Street.

　　　　　　　　And I remember
A fence of cardinals in Alabama, the snow, as
White and wide as a desert dream, at Montpelier.

The moonlit beach of Florida, the flaming Catskills
At Dover in the fall, and these cities of one night:
Raleigh, Hartford, Canton, Nashville, Northampton,
Portsmouth—havens of my love.

                    And I remember
Too, with old inquietude, the empty years, the long
    despondency
Of the sheepish time, the lonely and frightening war,
The devastation of divorce—wild love, searching. These
Were times to study good endeavor, had one the fortitude.

All, all shaped to love. Convexly and concavely. Rounded
Inward or outward. Bless you, darlings, for your favors.
Curse you, curse you doubly for your infidelities.
As I am cursed.

             No, there's a better cause, an apter
And deeper impetus to tragedy. To be true is
To hold to an old ideal only, the stone of sentiment,
Not the living flesh that curves and melts and quivers
With deep rage. The hurt is love, the ravage is
An outcome of right action. Quick and angry, I
Struck down all my beautiful sisters, who had looked
Past my shoulder, and they were unhurt; but they fell
Into heaps of cracked bones when I picked them up.
Dear ones, restrain your guilt. We have striven too much
For one another's comfort. Think of the world of
Saxifrage and sea urchin, panda and camelopard—
The ones crazier than we yet easy to conscience.
To know makes this seasickness, but to be wise
Is to accept the moon, the tides, we creatures swimming
There. To speak our needs, to say our love, to break
Every moment of another's silence with a word of our
Own desire—this is not cruelty but the saving way.

It is not love we lack, but understanding of the other,
And always will.

Lovers are changelings, never knowing
Whose lost blood pulses in their marvelous hearts.

I

Intent on love, I gave
Myself to mortal crime
And tried with love to save
The moments of love's time.
Time conquered and the course
Of marriage was divorce.

The earth's uncoiling years
Make a diverging span;
In each peeled hour appears
The poor, essential man;
At last he sees the source
Of being in divorce.

In every act I see
The austerity of loss:
Man's need is to be free;
His means escape; his cross
The life of his remorse.
The crisis is divorce.

Hands tore the tree, the bloom,
And cast us under earth;
The same hands rip the womb
At our own bloody birth.
In agony we force
The sundering divorce.

59

We can no easier stay
The quick, instinctive rent
Than we can stop the day
Of utmost ravishment.
Time's old assured recourse
Is, first and last, divorce.

Yet who would not succeed
And slow the knife of time,
Knitting his equal need
For love? Is this the crime,
A pure faith luring coarse
And snickering divorce?

Yes, but the blood and nerve
Confirm a human fate,
To love and to observe
Love grow complex with hate.
Defeated, we endorse
The desperate divorce.

Later, stripped and alone,
When we had hoped for strength,
In sorrow we atone
For weakness and time's length.
We lose our last resource,
Our object, in divorce.

The weak are the depressed,
The free are the forsaken.
How quickly they detest
The freedom they have taken.
Listen, wild and hoarse,
The lonely damn divorce.

Swept by aimless winds,
As if on a murderous sea,

I cursed love that rescinds
Its root in charity.
This was my dark discourse
On time and on divorce.

II

The struggle to achieve
A being good and free,
The labor to believe
A bestial pedigree,
From these our love withdraws,
Yet these contain our cause.

I said the fight is won
By those who know the joy
Of fighting all alone.
I said I would destroy
The insubstantial gauze
Of love that wrapped my cause.

Betrayal is a kiss,
Weakness is a touch;
Much better to dismiss
The hands that take too much.
Caressing hands are claws
That rip the tender cause.

In halls of printed ink,
The chambers of old friends,
I came well filled with drink
To make a new amends.
My manner drew applause,
But I forgot my cause.

My antics were like clouds
Of violent tenuous shapes;
Amid diaphanous crowds
I leapt for public grapes.
Alas, my foxy jaws
Snapped short of a living cause.

I felt my arms grow long,
I felt my head grow high,
My laughter waxed more strong,
Inventions filled my eye.
Others discerned the flaws
That tokened my lost cause.

Without a sanction in faith
Or a purpose in history,
Can a man be more than wraith
Or less than monstrosity?
I cried for absolute laws
To suppress a human cause.

First was the little pang,
The moment of unease.
The red-winged blackbird sang
Upon the queer March breeze.
It was the sunlit pause
Before the shattering cause.

Then summer wrung us dry.
In sweat I kept my bed,
Hearing my hollow lie
Cook in my hollow head.
I knew that nothing gnaws
The heart like one's old cause.

Wholeness I pondered. Hate
I knew, and needful love.
And how could I create
A life from these? Above
The town where the wind saws
I went and mourned my cause.

III

To accept the ache of love,
Ignore the ache of want,
To know the limit of
A thought, and bear the brunt
Of ignorance is what's meant
By being self-content.

I dreamt I lived by the sea
And made poor poems there,
And sea-birds came to me
And stood about my chair.
And in that parliament,
Speaking, I was content.

Again, I lived in the woods
And worked in the shade of trees,
Scheming rare livelihoods
For my unprosperous ease;
Friend to the oak that lent
Its shade to my content.

Such dreaming tells me this:
Only the heart can yield
A consummate synthesis
Of the plow and the unplowed field,

The world and a sentiment.
This is our content.

No freedom can assure
The freedom to be free;
Freedom must be impure
For freedom first to be;
In a choice of prisonment
One purposes content.

Let love flow back and lift
My being with the rest
Where self becomes the gift
I give to be possessed.
Thence, selfless but unspent,
Let me achieve content.

The garden was despoiled,
And yet we live in it;
Many lovers have toiled
That it should be thus fit
For our environment
In seasons of content.

The summer of my thirst,
My term of dying, may
Perhaps become the first
Gift I can give away,
Thus my ingredient
In everyone's content.

The free are the engaged;
The captive is serene.
Lovers who were enraged
Perceive an unforeseen

Rebirth and increment
Of love in new content.

The red-winged blackbird's song
Is heard again, again
And life seems very long.
I wait my season. Then
The blackbirds will present
My summer of content.

Envoi

The sun returns perforce,
Time's lenient measure thaws
Our wintry element.
For time is a long divorce
And a long, long quest for cause
That leads us to content.
But wounds are many, the wounded shy,
And many, many the ones who die.

1

Lovers are changelings, never knowing whose lost blood
Pulses in their marvelous hearts. Even a little upward glance
Of a tipsy, flirtatious, tenebrous eye, in the suddenly
Darling head of the wife of a friend, may be
The arrow of old pain shooting through the years to
Its quivering mark in the eye of my first, first love.
We fuse, we blur, in and out of one another's arms,
Merging, making our soft histories, running like blood
Through the channeling veins of our memories and our
Desires. Ah, who? Mother? Daughter? Cousin? Speak!
Say your lineage in my love. You do not know,
And seldom do I know, for the first love is before
Time, so long ago, there in the back of the cave,

The pristine secret dark joy. Then months and years
Tumble down the cascade of life and break like lumber
On the rock of the immoveable present, throwing up
Repeated shapes, over and over. Once, coming down
Suddenly into the valley of the Delaware on a day
Late in April, I was with the old Jews, come to their
Land at last. My own life—what is it but the
Experience of that certain wart I wear? And you,
My lovers, am I not the flicker of an old dream behind
Your eyes? Lovers are changelings, never knowing
Whose lost blood pulses in their marvelous hearts.

Wherefore, on a day in November, a day when the sky
Was its deepest blue and sunlight dazzled the eye
Like a rain of jewels, I hied me a second time to church
And there a second time espoused a wife. Manhattan
Shone, glass and steel making many facets, and the air
Sang. I wambled, stabbed by light at the temple's nerves,
Stung, jittery, tight-toothed to pursue the new esperance
Through any day's hell. Relatives jigging their smiles, damn
Them all, and a latitudinarian exercise during which the
Progifolly divulged that eximious sonnet of Shakespeare's,
And I wished they'd both succumbed in their cradles.
Champagne, the ceremonial water, completed the occasion,
Or rather its public aspect, but failed to modify the
Impression of sand in my mouth. Having twice enacted
The lesser of the principal roles in these solemnities, I
Speak with a certain conviction when I say there must be
An easier way to accomplish what is after all
In the nature of things. The usual defense is aliunde,
A theanthropic view, persuasive, lovely, but algoric
To the chief corneous intent. Puff-puff.

                                        Thence into the
Blue afternoon, into the secrecy of the New England
Hills, we drove, silent and content, in the snug car,

And as dusk fell on the woods and filled the valley of
The Housatonic, the year's first snow came, dancing
In the air before us, whitening the woods, swirling on
The crooked roadway, an assurance of privacy and our
Inner joy, the weaving of the old tapestry of our
Dream. After my havoc, I sought, like the blind mole
Turning and gauging soft earth among the stones,
A residue of life in the broken circumstances, a place
For life's circuitous flow once more in love and peace.
We drove. A twisting way, to the village, the inn, the night
Of the wedded; and on again, back again, wedded,
Strong in love for the hard works of enduring, surviving.
A home was made; the accumulation of belongings began.
Love's quick understanding grew—a touch, a glance,
The language of secrets. We inhabited marriage, each
Other; we made of ourselves cities to protect us
From the great city without. Raids and forays
We made, arm in arm, and at our own fire we were
Wise in our councils, calm, and our bread was eaten
With radical piety. Our wine was of poverty, drunk
Joyously. But evil lived. The worm made himself known
Within, insistently; the sea within sloped and narrowed
And poured stormily.

                    In less than one year, in only
Eight months, disaster and havoc fell on me again. Again!
Madness and sequestration. Now I have been
Separate from my wife almost as long as I was with her.

        It was a doomed chance
        now I see, taken
        in the maddening boughs
        of an autumn tree
        as the leaves fell quickly,
        denuding me. Thickly

my love made dance
when the fears were shaken,
but then came the rain.
The master of any house
he enters is pain,
the robber, and his glance
and his thieving ways
create the loveless days.
He absorbs all words
in silence, and all love,
as the summer tree
acquires the birds
when storm breaks above.
The storm is the stain
spreading over the room,
hiding the people in gloom.
Now here guilt storms.
It is dangerous, beloved, yet
genuine to abet
my despair. I have lost
your way; where you have lain
is nowhere, yonder
in my past wonder.
Now the heavy cost
drains me, kills me. Ever
in this after I discover
only the need under
each hammering blow,
and all seeking never
discloses the way of a lover.
Such is my pain.
Lower, lower, deep head,
pray for forgiveness,
pray for the cold snow
to cover the blood

suddenly.
All that I said
I shall utter again.
Pain is my master,
love is my sorrow,
hate my disaster,
loneliness my tomorrow.
My darling, my dear,
what will be next year?
The year after?
Deep, deep disease
betrays me, a long betrayal
lasting beyond my best denial,
and now you are its seize,
its murder, its urge,
unwittingly. I long for laughter,
for our dream of a gay
uncontainable day.
Again, again, again,
at the soft moment when
a whole true word was spoken
the soul's gate was broken.
In the deathward surge
the losses multiply,
the wreckage mounts high,
all of us skewered and strewn.
But for you, my innocent,
my heart is slow, slow,
my tears are penitent.
I commune
with our old hero
sadly and bid him go.

Loss, lost—the word that tells. Time is attrition. All
Our bulwarks crumble away, leaving us vulnerable,

Our possessions disappear, leaving us poor; and, in
That saintlike condition, we find no stalwart
But only the ragged weakling, unable to help himself.
Such deprivations cannot be compensated. To learn
Is to know finally weakness and fallibility and hate.
Love is a work of art, fit occupation for rare moods
And easily burned, cracked, torn, denounced by critics.

Of what consequence is this to the agglomerating
Giglots and dizzards out there?

                              Yes, this yip, this
Articulate squeak has been a very little noise
Amid the universal sunderings and explosions.
Bikini—is it gone yet? Forever? Where is Brooklyn?

My descent is only two hundred generations from
Those recognizable people who first dreamt
Of making a permanent mark, theopolitans who began
This agonizing history. I, Magister Artium,
Cannot adduce a lineage either long or illustrious;
Eons (time measured by the draining of the seas)
Before us, and perhaps the eons after, the grand schemes
Displace; think of the diastrophic dance. Even now
The thoughtless undercurrent animates us: my poor
Alien daughter lives, a functional unit of cells
So organized as to be of this species, perpetuating
Our two-legged kind in spite of all this wailing
And gnashing of teeth. Our agons and agues, what
Can they be in this huge history but the shames of our
Recusancy, the fidgets of our boredom. The skies,
Plicate and infinite, enfold us, and we dream that
Hurtling Jupiter is friendly, that Castor and Pollux
Lean familiarly over the night; all a pavane, we
Say. Metagalactic wastes, itinerant combustions,

70

Fissions and fusions more horrible than hell, whirling,
Burning—are these the dimensions of our uneasy love?

It must be so. Rocking and careening through the realms
Of action, we are the same old thoughtless creatures, versed
Intuitively in the anxious blow, the casual murder.
And the vermicular appendage spurts carelessly; it is
Proteiform, flexuous, blind. The trembling vessel gapes,
Clutches, sucks, subsides. We tramp to our knees
In the seed of all living things, spilling our own as we go,
Our heads truly in the clouds. Our faces are a cloud,
Shifting, dispersing, vacuous, blown over the world, and only
Down below do the animals scurry to undo our errors.

No, I find not comfort in these thoughts, but sorrow,
Deep sorrow, for I must crush this world that is all my love.

> For thon demgeorne dreorigne oft
> In hyra breostcofan bindath fæste.

The gathering fog closes. Rust,
The winter's disease, spreads
Like a cloak of blood on the metal.
Little waves stir under the wharf.
Only the terns work, plying
A swift traffic outward and inward.

The bell-buoy chimes in the harbor,
January's song, and the fog is cold.
We fear the coming of ice to our harbor.

One has spoken to me of conflict.
He has scarred my mind with his voice.
His hands made structures in the air.
Somehow he has found an old diary
I wrote and had forgotten,

Stiff pages and a childish scrawl.
Of provenance he spoke, and growth,
And he told me in his soft voice
Of the wasted years, the losses
Mounting when I strove and loved.
I listened, too weary to protest.

Vanity hath betrayed me.
Yes, I dreamt of deeds.
I ventured, I journeyed.
I dreamt of the love of fair ladies.
I found them, I wore their scarves.
My dreaming, hours by the iris when sun
Awakened the marshland
And the red-winged blackbird sang,
Were the attainable contentment,
Had I been content. Vanity hath
Destroyed me, fierce seignior.
Thy will hath destroyed me.

Striving for goodness against
The evil within me,
Striving for love against
The hatred within me,
Striving for peace against
The hunger within me,
I waged honorable war.

I am the victor. I established
The right. My spoils were sorrow.

As a great nation wars,
Mustering all citizens and all wealth,
To rescue those who are truly
Pitiable, even at the expense

Of many lives, of anguish, perhaps
Of smaller nations; so the
Individual makes conquest
Of himself, coercing the base animal
To right action, and the victory
Destroys his fortitude, his balance,
And perhaps those he has loved.

Retreat. Pray for forgiveness.

All you whom I have violated
Out of your great goodness forget me.
You whom I have destroyed . . .

Remember, we concurred, we agreed.

After the battle the wounded rest,
And useless honor is accorded them.

This was the andantino.
   Speak no more of love and death
   And put away your sorrow:
   He who suffers is bound to know
   An empty heart tomorrow.

1

In deep winter the sea roams
Menacingly under the fog.
It roars through the quick gaps in the whiteness,
Then is muffled again.
Icebergs may loom, waves of mountainous force,
Ghosts may inhabit the fog.

The anchor-chain creaks.
The terns cry in the fog,

Voices of distress, dying.
A flower of drenched feathers
Comes in on the sloping tide.
The sea gives us many mementoes.

Memories circle and sweep outward and die.
Each tide brings to this harbor
Many corpses. And the harbor folk
Give flowers to the sea,
Wreathes flung to the vagrant waves.

On this ship the rust grows
Like moss on a ledge by the forest.
Fog lies on the sea and the deck.
Sound of lapping water, sound
Of rats' teeth busy. Candles
Saved from their ravening
Illumine a white face.

Shuffle, deal. Patience by candlelight.
The world rocks on the swinging sea.

*

HALL FIVE

The window bars are spider webs
  Where live our ancient folk,
The clock no longer keeps the time
  And chimes with a random stroke.

The faces gathered in that gloom
  Are often wet with tears
For joy and melancholy rise
  Quickly at ninety years.

74

And Georgie beats the tom-tom, Dick
   Draws horsies in the dust,
And Buddy Boy from San Antone
   Sings songs of his deep disgust.

The millionaire looks up, surprised
   That this should come to men,
And cries until the nurse can come
   And make him dry again.

The Palace of the Doges hangs,
   A tinted photograph,
Above the broken lamp that looks
   Like a tumbledown giraffe.

The boo lives under the billiard table
   And makes his gentle moan,
At night the wambus flies the hall
   Where he has always flown.

So much has been forgotten that
   We sometimes think perhaps
They have forgotten everything,
   But no, the little lapse

From dreaming lets a memory in,
   And then the old men swoon
And say, "Dear friend, come easily,
   And please, dear friend, come soon."

◆

WORDS FOR MY DAUGHTER

Alas, that earth's mere measure strains our blood
And makes more airy still this parentage.

The bond is all pretending, and you sleep
When my affections leap
And gasp at old hope vainly in my night's cage.

Dear marvelous alien snippet, yes, you move
Like a down-raining cloud in my mind, a bird
Askim on low planes under lightning thought,
An alter-image caught
In gossamer seed, my most elusive word.

There must be some connection, more than mood,
The yearning wit of loneliness, and more
Than meets the law on that certificate.
Strangers do not create
Alliances so deep and dark and sore.

Yet we are strangers. I remember you
When you began, a subtle soft machine;
And you remember me, no, not at all;
Or maybe you recall
A vacancy where someone once was seen.

I can address you only in my mind,
Or, what's the same, in this untouching verse.
We are the faceless persons who exist
Airily, as a gist
Of love to warp the loves that we rehearse.

Strangers we are, a father and a daughter,
This Hayden and this Martha. And this song,
Which turns so dark when I had meant it light,
Speaks not at all of right
And not at all, since they are dim, of wrong.

Distance that leaves me powerless to know you
Preserves you from my love, my hurt. You fare

Far from this room hidden in the cold north;
Nothing of me goes forth
To father you, lost daughter, but a prayer.

That some small wisdom always may endure
Amidst your weariness; that lovers may
Be kind to you; that beauty may arouse
You; that the crazy house
May never, never be your home: I pray.

November to January, 1953-54